Scar Tissue

poems by

Eve Rifkah

Finishing Line Press
Georgetown, Kentucky

Scar Tissue

Copyright © 2017 by Eve Rifkah
ISBN 978-1-63534-239-0 First Edition
All rights reserved under International and Pan-American Copyright Conventions. No part of this book may be reproduced in any manner whatsoever without written permission from the publisher, except in the case of brief quotations embodied in critical articles and reviews.

ACKNOWLEDGMENTS

I wish to thank Kenneth Kamiel for his support throughout this project.

Publisher: Leah Maines

Editor: Christen Kincaid

Cover Art: Victor Israel Bravman

Author Photo: Betty Jenewin

Cover Design: Colin Sjostedt

Printed in the USA on acid-free paper.
Order online: www.finishinglinepress.com
          also available on amazon.com

Author inquiries and mail orders:
Finishing Line Press
P. O. Box 1626
Georgetown, Kentucky 40324
U. S. A.

Table of Contents

Scar Tissue 1
Not Mother Not Daughter 2
Rosary 3
Stepmother 4
Birth Mother 5
In the Stepmother's House 6
Cora's Not Crazy 7
Corrella 8
Cora and Brother 9
Shock Treatment 10
RN 11
Cora and Me Last Time 12
The Wedding 14
Marriage Bed 15
Births and Deaths 16
Cora Goes to Work 18
Craziness Erupts in Unexpected Quarters 19
Pastel Portrait 20
Home Nurse 21
Youngest Child Briefly Finds Beauty 22
Visit 23
Cora Laughs 24
After Brother's Death 25
She Talks 26
I Call 27
Cora Decides Enough Is Enough 28

In memory of
Corinne Green Bravman Kamiel
1925-2014

Scar Tissue

all above the table   invisible
foster mother/not mother tied up with dinner
foster sisters/not sisters setting table
arms overhead   rustle
and slap   the teapot set down
way up on top   little one
     grabs and yanks
cloth in tight fists

pot   dishes   silver
slow slide   quick pour
all that hot   soaks Cora's dress
scream and howl
mother not mother rushes and
grabs tiny girl   rips open all the tiny buttons
pulls cloth away   skin steamed scarlet

at the hospital nurses without smiles
without a soft word take over
days into months
scold skin   rip and patch
glazed over   armor hard
one arm never the same

Not Mother Not Daughter

the father comes with a woman in tow
holds her elbow
this is your daughter
he points to baby Cora
NO, I have no daughter
Not mine   she screams
father rips her away
cries bounce off the walls
the door frame   roll down the street

later sister/not sister says your motherlady beautiful
hair like mahogany
like bureau and bed

Rosary

father came   stiff and proper
a bitten smile tightens his lips
mother not mother hugs and smiles
straightens her dress

In the car Cora shows father how
she can recite the rosary   stringing
pretend beads through her fingers

anger strawberries father's face
no *goyem* words for you
no mother Mary   no Jesus
he sputters

Cora cringes inside pressed dress
perfect pleats not perfect anymore

Stepmother

in the foster home   Cora
the Jew outsider in the Catholic home
confession, communion, catechism
stuff the others do
Cora the different one
something about the man called father
one day he comes with another woman
corset held straight and hard
                    Cora feels
mean spirits fly from woman's eyes
feels hate   new word washes Cora in doom

she whispers   *don't like her*
woman in loud
voice of what is to come
I don't like you either

now bad dreams happen when eyes open

Birth Mother

the father said   dress in prettiest dress
Cora thinks party   thinks special
thinks exciting to go someplace unknown
in the black car   back seat next to real brother
        black hair   wrack of waves
contrast to her fair

at the brick building
    how lovely who lives here?
inside father pulls her to edge of
long box   a woman lies hard and still
your mother—look at her
no party this
hides head in hands
    look at her
at face like brother's
bustled by grownups dressed in dark
    no tears stain their faces
    no hugs for motherless child

at the cemetery, the rough-cut box
lowers by ropes into the raw earth

brother mourns forever
cross to bear

In the Stepmother's House

the rubber tree touches the ceiling
is cut down to make another
green leaves spike and unravel
on sills and narrow tables
nary a bloom to behold.
flowers die, she says
as first husband did
while second daughter still inside
snagged herself a second
who always held a job.

she bought pawned Dresden figurines
fragile porcelain cups and saucers.
he bought clocks wound by day, by week.
always food on the table,
silverware poked in potted plants
cleansed in the only earth they had
every bite kosher, slow chewed to the tocking of time.

Cora's Not Crazy

        though scared   through life
not crazy   *won't be crazy*   *not crazy*
everyday mantra in that house
father and stepmother
wait for signs
watch every movement every word
every down-casting eye
every run-and-hide
everywhere
they watch and wait
        mother's craziness
birthed in child

when Cora is engaged
father asks brother
tell her not to wed   not to
make more craziness
brother for once   disobeys
no nun-life for her

Corrella

The stepmother's daughters perfect
born of first husband
one golden haired   one dark and meek
every week Cora polishes the teak table
brought from China by the traveling uncle not uncle
dragons carved to kill
     brass table top incised in pain
Cora rubs and rubs   hands raw
back aches   rubs brass into gold

all the chores fall on her head
tears held clenched
fall hard inside   hot black cinders
etch pale designs
hides spells and curses

Cora and Brother

                    hold hands
bolster against witch of mean
and the witch's brother's eyes see through stone
from his tongue
                parasites of pain
the brother and sister   leaking crumbs   lose their way
down steep hills and dead-end alleys
voices hound beyond the grave
stalk them all their days

RN

Cora carries memory
nurses' raw hands push
rough tongues scold
her skin rip and heal
rip and heal

Cora knows she will be a nurse
be kind   be gentle
graduation photo in starched white hat
black ribbon pinned to brim—
a handsome woman

war time hurt time
                    holes where flesh used to be
she tends the man with one leg one eye
not whole her father says
she marries anyway
at the wedding, they dance
husband on false leg sees beyond glass eye
carries crazy on his side too

Shock Treatment

stepmother tells Cora call in sick
Cora says nurses overworked can't cover
stepmother tells Cora no work today
no talking back to that woman

Cora cares for stepsister's baby
cleans house
the steps leave early morning
until late   never say where
some things not mentioned
though Cora a nurse

stepsister returns trembling head to foot
electricity   brain-shot
post-partum jolt
into awareness   to tend the child
         one of the special ones

Cora and Me Last Time

Cora swings me into the stroller
while our three-room belongings slide
three flights on men like ants descending
to the mouth of the truck

1952, the stroller is huge and heavy
Cora pushes me up Blue Hill Ave.
across the browning grass of Franklin Field
by the stone wall the big kids sit on

after *shul* on the high holidays
Cora is always happy
singing loud
we turn up Johnson Road
at number fifty Cora stops
pulls me up the stairs   more stairs
singing out *hellooooooo*

on the dark landing the landlady
opens her door and yells to
stop the noise   Cora's noise
in her hall   on her stairs

we tip-toe down to wait
oh, so quiet on the porch
for the truck with my father driving
to come up the road of look-alike houses
our things climb up with the movers

Cora left to nurse in Israel
the place we say next year in
but Cora doesn't wait
for a never next year

accepts the Hadassah money
to get away
lucky Cora

I'm scared again
each time I creep the stairs
past the landlady's door
alone

The Wedding

when Cora weds, I walked down that aisle
next to the perfect cross-eyed cousin
couldn't walk straight line   her pudgy body
held in pink satin
me trying to tiny step on edge of carpet
everyone looking
at that strap fallen on my arm
blue net scratching skin
heavy hair stick-straight wilted
in August heat after afternoon curling

we hold flower baskets with the flowers stuck in
unlike picture books where flower girls strew
petals over narrow carpet

I watched Cora dance away
to another state of mind
named Queens
me age five without anyone loving me
anymore

Marriage Bed

the forks lined up
with spoons and knives
plate a sullied moon

lip-curled bluster across restaurant table
glass-eye glints in candlelight
over done   tough   her fault
knees lost under white cloth shake
she rubs gold band with thumb
              married now

honeymoon   tipped over moon
honey spilled
August chill rises over rocks   she climbs
to somewhere else   nowhere else
lie in bed made

this chosen one no better
all wanting and poking and chiding
all demand and smirk

a new name to sign now
the old bulges between
only RN at the end
shows who she is until the babies
come   one flaw after another.

Births and Loss

when a girl is born
Cora's father said name after mother
the woman seen only in death
Cora defies this time
names daughter for foster sister
but girl carries crazed genes
a torment forever
anger behind every
morning cloud   eats every dream alive

the second child comes
never to rollover to sit or speak
the doctor blamed—forceps birth
yanks into blankness
Cora holds and tends
boy heavier and heavier
when next pregnancy grows
she gives up child to hospital
until death ends breath in and out

third child born whole born scream
until grown he falls off edge of night
black wraps his limbs
descending to despair
every working day

another boy is born heart-holed
dies before spring   cold weakened
Cora's heart punctured again

as Cora ages a final son born early
never quite right in body
turns to rituals of prayer
follows the torah
Cora learns again about kosher
whatever left behind taken up
in spades
the way it is
just the way it is

Cora Goes to Work

as a school nurse
when others retire
traveling by bus and subway
car or cab
around the city   Queens, Bronx, Brooklyn
hands out sanitary napkins
to girls caught unprepared
lets them skip classes
rest in nurse's office
hands out the meds that calm the hypers
bouncing in and out
Cora gentle and kind
forced out at eighty-two
now worries about bills
as her children nickel and dollar her
crazy skips generation comes back
flies in her face pecks at her eyes

Cora still whispers   *not crazy*
not crazy

Craziness Erupts in Unexpected Quarters

the sister not sister   the daughter born of death
birthed a daughter tormented by demon
tongues wracked and weathered without wit
or reason turned day to night
to mares flying across arcing skies
fear twists the reins tighter than hospital doors
as drugs to quiet the voices eat her insides to death

Pastel Portrait

after the parents die the real and the step
Cora takes the pastel portrait the brother
drew in art school after the war
Cora so pretty
golden hair in rough strokes
violet eyes precise
the brown paper shows through
Cora caught behind the glass
paper a solid sheet to lie on
grains of color merge into a face
and fall away
held tight in a frame
young forever

Home Nurse

husband falls down
says no more walking for me
removes the false leg
heavy straps that wrapped his thigh
moves from wheelchair to bed
                    and back again
      all day long days
Cora at beck and call
for every little thing
husband whines
            Cora this and Cora that

Cora's Youngest Briefly Finds Beauty

this child/man   pale and soft   *davening* prayers
asks God for a wife while perusing the personals
travels up and down the coast seeking the one
who won't turn away
falls in love with the woman
carrying illness from birth
marries by God but not by state
the second-year wife falls into sleep
three months while prayers ascend
God kisses awake   a miracle the rabbi father says
but even miracles fade
at *Pesach* no lamb blood smeared over hospital door
beauty sleeps into death
Cora says best this way

Visit

I take Cora to the Metropolitan
this woman fifty-five years in NYC
never stepped foot inside
now stunned by beauty
walking by Central Park
surprised by trees she never walked under
Cora lived sheltered by fear
never crossed bridges or took subway underground
in the hospital that still tends the lepers
I read my poems of long ago lepers

at the end of *Shabos* we eat kosher Chinese
as son buys palm leaf—*lulah* and *etrog*
in the cramped apartment lost to light
every surface drowned in paper, boxes, kitsch
sugar spilled never swept away
the fattest cat in the world
holds dominion
there is nothing
        I can do

Cora Laughs

        over a jar of peanut butter
found in her stepsister's apartment

over her stepmother long gone
name sticks in her mouth
hand half hides
You know who
Minnie, I say, like Minnie Mouse

She laughs when I call
at all the harsh memories
and the sweet

it is what it is
she says of anything
what can you do?

After Brother's Death

every week they talked
Cora and my dad
sometimes she heard Nel in the background
haranguing   then call cut short
he only spoke of landscapes,
weather, garden planted,
beautiful things
never said anything
of the beatings,
the threats of murder
she did this? Cora asks

She Talks

on the phone
tells the same stories
brother helped with homework
one day ran away got as far as Natick
called home
his tormentor not-uncle retrieved him
never tried again
left when drafted to enter
fears never spoken
went to art school without a degree
married the one he got with child
but it couldn't be, Cora says
I tell her of the child
lost before my birth
on the phone
lost secrets rattle the wires
shaking between us

I Call

Aunt it's Eve

she begins litany of recent disasters
the hospital, rehab, hospital, rehab
now home   visiting nurse
not right yet   but better

I interject
        my voice lost in her run of words
Cora, I say
        Listen
she says
        Thanks for calling
        I'll keep in touch
my words circle the room
        inhale back into throat
chest   stomach

who am I?
        fragments
    scatter in all directions

    pieces big enough to
        fall through

Cora Decides Enough is Enough

On Rosh Hashanah Cora steps
into the air   nothing holds
she tumbles and spills ….

in the hospital, the nurse turned patient
smiles at the nurses
tables reversed   wants to book it out of there

balks at rehab
knows too much

decides to leave the only way out
stops eating   then refuses to wake
doctors advise   rabbi agrees
tells sons to let go
God can't heal an old lady
seeking peace
at last

Eve Rifkah grew up in Dorchester, MA when the scent of chocolate filled the air on cloudy days. Although Rifkah never spent time in foster care as did her Aunt Corinne, portrayed in *Scar Tissue*; she often wished she could be adopted. At 19 Rifkah dropped out of college to have a child and a brief marriage. At 50 she married again and continued her formal education to earn a MFA from Vermont College of Fine Arts. After a lifetime of blue collar jobs this entitled her to work as an adjunct professor until teaching positions vanished. She now calls herself retired as it sounds better then unemployed.

Rifkah loves history and doing research hence, her first book *Outcasts the Penikese Leper Hospital 1905-1921* (Little Pear Press, 2010) documents the lives and times of a barely known leper colony off the coast of Massachusetts. Her second book *Dear Suzanne* (WordTech Communications, 2010), is on the life of model and artist Suzanne Valadon, 1865-1938.

Eve Rifkah was co-founder of Poetry Oasis, Inc. (1998-2012), a non-profit poetry association dedicated to education and promoting local poets. She was founder, editor and chief cook and bottle-washer of the literary magazine DINER (2001-2007). Rifkah is also a quilt maker and fabric artist.

She lives in Worcester, MA with her husband and cat.

www.ingramcontent.com/pod-product-compliance
Lightning Source LLC
LaVergne TN
LVHW041513070426
835507LV00012B/1538